KIDS' DAY OUT

Playgrounds and Adventure Parks

Joanne Mattern

RED
CHAIR
•PRESS•

Kids' Day Out is produced and published by Red Chair Press:

Red Chair Press LLC   PO Box 333   South Egremont, MA 01258-0333

www.redchairpress.com

Publisher's Cataloging-In-Publication Data

Names: Mattern, Joanne, 1963–

Title: Playgrounds and adventure parks / Joanne Mattern.

Description: Egremont, MA : Red Chair Press, [2018] | Series: Kids' day out | Interest age level: 007-010. | Includes index and glossary. | Summary: "When you hear the word 'playground,' what do you think of? Do you picture slides and swings? Do you think of climbing walls and tunnels? Or do you picture pirate ships and space to run? Over the years, playgrounds have changed in many ways. But they have always been a place where children can enjoy themselves and learn important lessons about safety and getting along with others. Discover how playgrounds came to be and how they have changed over the years!"--Provided by publisher.

Identifiers: ISBN 978-1-63440-389-4 (library hardcover) | ISBN 978-1-63440-393-1 (ebook)

Subjects: LCSH: Playgrounds--History--Juvenile literature. | CYAC: Playgrounds--History.

Classification: LCC GV423 .M38 2018 (print) | LCC GV423 (ebook) | DDC 796.068--dc23

Photo credits: p. 6, 7, 8, 9, 10, 11,12, 14, 15, 16, 30, 31, Library of Congress; p. Cover, 3, 4, 20, 26, 27: iStock; p. 1, 18, 19, 20, 21, 22, 25, 29: Dreamstime; p. 17, 23, 24, 27, 28: Alamy

Printed in the United States of America

0518 1P CGBF18

Contents

ong ago, children did not need playgrounds. Most people lived in rural areas. Even big cities had open spaces. Children had plenty of room to run and play.

During the 1800s, more people moved to cities to work in new factories there. Living conditions were very crowded. Soon there were no open places where children could play. Instead, they played in the street. But the streets were not safe places to play.

Contents

Let's Play!

When you hear the word "playground," what do you think of? Do you picture slides and swings? Do you think of climbing walls and tunnels? Or do you picture pirate ships and space to run?

A playground can be many kinds. Some playgrounds have lots of equipment. Others have open space and places to use your imagination. Over the years, playgrounds have changed in many ways. But they have always been a place where children can enjoy themselves and learn important lessons about getting along with others. Let's go back and look at how playgrounds came to be and how they have changed over the years.

No Place to Play

Long ago, children did not need playgrounds. Most people lived in rural areas. Even big cities had open spaces. Children had plenty of room to run and play.

During the 1800s, more people moved to cities to work in new factories there. Living conditions were very crowded. Soon there were no open places where children could play. Instead, they played in the street. But the streets were not safe places to play.

In 1848, a man named Henry Barnard drew the first known picture of a playground. His drawing showed a large area with toys and swings. Adults watched the children play. However, the first playground was not built until 1859. That playground was in a park in the city of Manchester, England.

The first playground in the United States opened in San Francisco's Golden Gate Park in 1887. It had swings, slides, and a

carousel. However, other cities did not follow San Francisco's lead. No more playgrounds were built for many years.

During the late 1800s and early 1900s, millions of immigrants came to the United States. Many lived in dirty slums in crowded cities. Social reformers believed that children needed clean, safe places to play. They also believed that playgrounds could help immigrants learn about the American way of life. Learning to play together would teach children and their families American traditions and values. The reformers said playgrounds would also improve children's health by providing fresh air and exercise.

In 1898, a group called the Outdoor Recreation League donated slides and seesaws to New York City. The equipment was placed in small parks in run-down neighborhoods. In 1903, the city of New York built its first playground. It was called Seward Park. Seward Park had a slide and a sandbox.

A Place to Play—and Learn

In 1906, the Playground Association of America was formed. This group worked to have playgrounds in all major cities. Over the next ten years, playgrounds were built all over the country. These playgrounds were not just for children. Teachers worked at the playgrounds. They taught children how to use the equipment. They showed them how to play together and take turns. They led parades and other family activities in the playgrounds.

Even President Theodore Roosevelt thought playgrounds were a good idea. In 1907, he gave a speech that said, "City streets are unsatisfactory playgrounds for children because of the danger...and because in crowded sections of the city they are apt to be schools of crime....Since play is a fundamental need, playgrounds should be provided for every child as much as schools."

Tall and Scary!

The playgrounds of the early 1900s looked very different than playgrounds do today. The main feature of these playgrounds was called the apparatus. The apparatus was a tall metal or wooden structure. It had several different areas. Children could swing from bars or rings. They could slide down very steep slides. They could climb ladders that leaned against the frame.

It's a Fact

The apparatus was not just for children. Adults could use it too! Playgrounds were often lit at night so adults could use them after work.

Playgrounds of this time were not just a place to play. Playgrounds might also include a track for running. Some had fields where people could play ball games or plant gardens. Separate buildings could be used as theaters or libraries or even health clinics. Playgrounds were really community centers for the whole family.

The apparatus might have been fun to climb and play on, but it was also unsafe. In 1912, New York City banned all climbing structures in its playgrounds. After that, equipment such as seesaws, swings, and merry-go-rounds was more common. There were still monkey bars and things to climb on, but they were much smaller and not as high.

One popular piece of equipment was called the giant stride. The giant stride was a tall pole. Long ropes hung down from the center of the pole, and there was a ring or a metal ladder on the end of each rope. Children could hold on to the ring or ladder and swing quickly around the pole. Like many pieces of playground equipment from this time, the giant stride was exciting but dangerous!

Adventure Playgrounds

By the 1930s, playgrounds had changed from community centers to play areas. A playground of this time had many different pieces of equipment. Most were made of metal and heavy wood. There were no adults to teach children or lead them in play.

In 1931, a Danish architect named Carl Theodor Sorensen noticed something. Children were more interested in playing with empty boxes than they were in enjoying his playgrounds. Sorensen got an idea. He built the first junk playground. Later, these playgrounds were called adventure playgrounds.

An adventure playground usually has
large boxes or metal tubes. The playground
might also include old tires, telephone poles,
or pieces of recycled wood or metal. These
playgrounds encouraged children to use
their imagination. The playground could be
whatever they wanted it to be.

In 1965, two architects designed a New York City playground that featured slides that children could climb or roll down instead of just sliding on.

Use Your Imagination!

After World War II ended in 1945, people built new kinds of playgrounds. Like adventure playgrounds, these areas encouraged children to use their imagination. Artists designed playgrounds that featured odd shapes and designs. Many playgrounds featured sculptures of dragons, dinosaurs, and animals. Others had pirate ships or space ships. Some looked like castles or cowboy towns in the Old West.

Slides and climbing walls were connected with pathways and ladders. Children could move all over the equipment and imagine different games and scenes. Instead of metal, some playgrounds used sand to create different areas where children could play.

During the 1980s, people were worried about playground safety. They said playgrounds had a lot of problems. They said children could be hit by wooden swings, seats or chains or fall off high slides. Children could pinch their fingers or become caught in metal bars. They could get cuts or splinters playing on wooden equipment. If a child fell on the hard asphalt under the equipment, he or she could get hurt as well.

Parents demanded safer playgrounds. In time, the government passed laws stating what kind of equipment could be used on a playground. Equipment was made of plastic instead of metal or wood. Swings had cloth or rubber seats. Instead of a hard surface, the area under the equipment was made of softer material like shredded tires or soft rubber pieces.

How to Build a Playground

Playgrounds might look different today than they did one hundred years ago, but they are still great places to play. Many communities and schools build new playgrounds every year.

It takes a lot of work to build a playground. Members of the community meet to discuss what kind of playground they want. What equipment will the playground have? What will it look like? How big will it be? Communities often  have to raise money to build new playgrounds.

Once the community has raised the money and decided what to build, a playground construction company brings in the equipment. The company builds the playground. It puts down a soft surface underneath the equipment. The company must follow lots of rules to make sure the playground is safe.

Kids can help build playgrounds too! Some communities ask children for their ideas. Children are asked to use their imagination to create their dream playground. They can choose the equipment, the colors, and anything else they want.

After all the ideas are gathered, people vote on the best ideas. Then the community raises money. They might hold car washes or bake sales. They might have a special event like a basketball game and give the money to the playground fund.

Finally, the community hires a company to design and build the equipment. Then the adults and children work together to build their dream playground. Working hard, they can often build a playground in just one or two days!

A company called KaBOOM! helps communities design, fund, and build playgrounds using community members as volunteers.

Playgrounds for Everyone

Today's playgrounds try to have something for everyone. Younger children can climb small hills and slide down smaller slides. Babies can swing in special seats that keep them safe. Older children can run, climb and jump on larger pieces of equipment.

It's a Fact

Some places even have playgrounds for older people! These fitness parks are found in many places in Europe and Asia. They have exercise equipment, walkways, and stationery bikes that help older people exercise and stay healthy.

Many playgrounds also allow children with different abilities to have fun. Special swings hold wheelchairs. Ramps and railings help children who have trouble walking or seeing. These inclusive playgrounds allow all children to play together and have fun.

Playgrounds have changed a lot in the past 150 years! Instead of tall, unsafe metal structures, today's playgrounds have safer equipment that can be enjoyed by everyone from babies to older adults. Children of all abilities can play together and enjoy many different activities.

Playgrounds are fun places to play and exercise. They are also a great place to make new friends. Children learn important skills as they play with other children, use their imaginations, and try new things. Playgrounds are important places in any community!

Glossary

apparatus a tall metal piece of equipment found on early playgrounds

architect a person who designs buildings

equipment machines or structures used for a purpose

immigrants people who come from another country to live in a new country

recreation games and activities for fun

reformers people who want to improve things

rural to do with the countryside

sculptures something carved or shaped out of stone, wood, metal, or plastic

slums overcrowded and poor neighborhoods

stationary staying in one place

Learn More in the Library

Books about Playgrounds

Bloom, Paul. *Rules on the Playground.* New York: Gareth Stevens Publishing, 2016.

Rosen, Michael J. *Let's Build a Playground.* Boston: Candlewick Press, 2013.

Index

About the Author

Joanne Mattern is the author of many nonfiction books for children. She enjoys writing about animals, history, and famous people and loves to bring science and history to life for young readers. Joanne lives in New York State with her husband, four children, and several pets and enjoys reading and music.